Gwynedd's Lost Railways

by

Alun Turner

0-6-0ST No. 1748, fitted with a snowplough, at Trawsfynydd Station.

Text © Alun Turner, 2003.
First published in the United Kingdom, 2003,
reprinted 2013
by Stenlake Publishing Ltd,
01290 551122
www.stenlake.co.uk

ISBN 9781840332599

The publishers regret that they cannot supply
copies of any pictures featured in this book.

PICTURE ACKNOWLEDGEMENTS

The publishers wish to thank the following for contributing photographs
to this book: John Alsop for the front cover and pages 1, 2, 5, 8, 9, 14, 15, 17,
19, 20, 27–30, 32–34, 36–42, 44–48 and the back cover; Richard Casserley for
pages 3, 4, 6, 10–13, 16, 18, 21 (both), 22, 24–26, 31 and 43; and Alun Turner
and the Welsh Highland Light Railway for pages 7, 23 and 35.

The 2-6-2T engine 'Russell' at Beddgelert Station.

INTRODUCTION

North Wales, and the Gwynedd area in particular, was never over-blessed with passenger carrying standard gauge railways, and this has made the loss of those railways that have vanished even harder to bear. Because of the mountainous terrain, most railways tended to be narrow gauge and were, at least initially, designed to carry freight, mostly slate, from the mountains where it was quarried to the coast. Later these railways developed passenger services, initially for quarry workers who lived close enough to the railway to travel in and out to work each day, and also for those who lived further away and who travelled in on a Monday and out on a Saturday afternoon, living in barracks at the quarries during the week.

Some of the lines, like the Ffestiniog Railway, went on to court holidaymakers with special excursions, becoming an advanced form of what they are today – tourist railways. One of these lines, the Welsh Highland Light Railway, was, apart from the freight traffic that made up the most lucrative part of its operations, open only for passengers during the summer months for most of its short life.

Probably the most missed of the standard gauge lines is the former Bangor – Caernarfon – Afon Wen line, which formed a link between the Cambrian Coast line and the North Coast line. Whereas once an inhabitant of Porthmadog, say, could board a train in his own town, change at Afon Wen and be in Bangor or Llandudno within perhaps an hour, today two or three buses are needed to get the passenger there in perhaps double or more of the time. Such is progress. Many schemes and plans to reinstate this line have been put forward, but with the gradual disappearance of its course under new road schemes (and in one length a narrow gauge tourist railway), and the 'town link' tunnel under Castle Square in Caernarfon (which linked the Bangor–Caernarfon line with the Caernarfon–Afon Wen & Caernarfon-Llanberis lines) becoming part of a scheme to relieve traffic through Caernarfon, hopes of restoration in any form must now be past.

Part of the Bala–Blaenau Ffestiniog line (latterly the LNWR) did survive, but only as a means to carry nuclear waste from Trawsfynydd Power Station and even this traffic ceased on 12 August 1995. The track is still in situ on this stretch, but unless a preservation society comes forward to take it over it cannot be long before its remains disappear completely. Indeed, this line is possibly unique in that closure of the original did not come as a result of falling traffic or the failure to attract passengers or the state of the line, but was closed when part of its trackbed was flooded in the building of the reservoir in the Trewern Valley and another part was needed to re-route a road around the reservoir.

Apart from North Devon, there is possibly nowhere else in Great Britain where you can travel so far without seeing a railway line, other than a narrow gauge preserved line or an old trackbed long disused.

Ynys Station, looking towards Bangor, 27 June 1956.

Bangor – Caernarfon

Passenger service withdrawn	05/01/1970	*Stations*	*Dates of opening and closure*
Distance	9 miles 228 yards	Menai Bridge	1858 – still in use on the
Companies	Chester & Holyhead Railway;		Holyhead – Chester line
	London & North Western;	Treborth *	1855 – 02/03/1959
	London, Midland & Scottish	Port Dinorwic	10/03/1852 – 12/09/1960
		Griffiths Crossing	1854 – 05/07/1937
* Temporarily closed between 1858 and 03/1859.		Caernarfon	01/07/1852 – 05/01/1970

Menai Bridge Station, looking towards Bangor, 12 August 1953.

This line was built in 1851, using the Bangor to Holyhead line as far as Menai Bridge and then (initially) a single track line (changed to double track in 1872) to a station at the northern end of Caernarfon. This eventually became the station for the Afon Wen and Llanberis branches after the construction of the 'Town Link' tunnel under Caernarfon's Castle Square in 1871. Starting in July 1852, freight services ran until August 1969, reopening between June 1970 and February 1972.

Port Dinorwic Station, looking towards Afon Wen, 24 August 1954.

Caernarfon – Afon Wen

Passenger service withdrawn	07/12/1964	*Stations*	*Dates of opening and closure*
Distance	18 miles 820 yards	Groeslon	14/09/1866 – 07/12/1964
Companies	Caernarfonshire Railway;	Penygroes	14/09/1866 – 07/12/1964
	London & North Western;	Pant Glas	12/1869 – 07/01/1957
	London, Midland & Scottish	Brynkir	02/09/1867 – 07/12/1964
		Ynys	01/07/1872 – 07/12/1964
Stations	*Dates of opening and closure*	Llangybi	05/12/1869 – 07/12/1964
Caernarfon (Pant)	14/09/1866 – 05/07/1870	Chwilog	02/09/1869 – 07/12/1964
Dinas Junction *	14/09/1877 – 10/09/1951	Afon Wen	02/09/1861 – 07/12/1964
Llanwda **	14/09/1877 – 07/12/1964		

Dinas Junction, looking north, 1934. The standard gauge line is on the left and the Welsh Highland narrow gauge line is on the right.

* Renamed Dinas after closure of the Welsh Highland Railway in 1937.   ** Originally named Pwllheli Road.

Groeslon Station, pictured sometime before 1911.

The Caernarfon to Afon Wen branch was built by the Caernarfonshire Railway from Pant, on the southern side of Caernarfon, to Afon Wen, a junction with the Cambrian line. In fact the Caernarfonshire line reached Afon Wen first, and initial services over the Cambrian line to Criccieth and Porthmadog were hauled by Caernarfonshire Railway trains, although driven by Cambrian drivers.

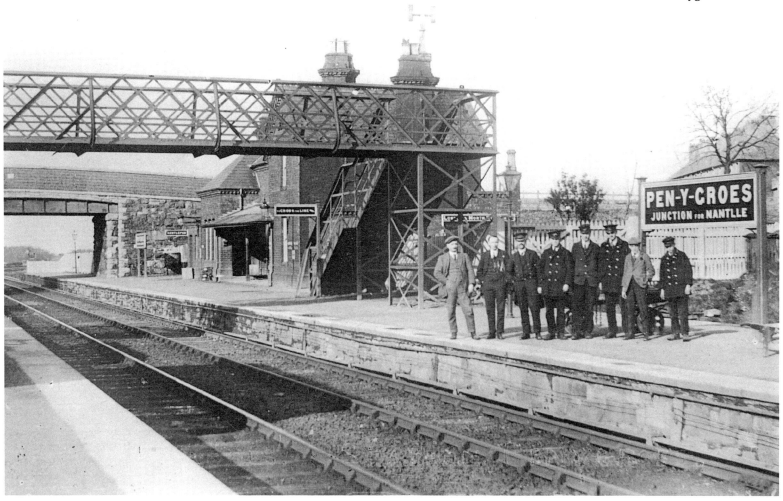

The route, as far as Penygroes, to a large extent followed the route of the earlier Nantlle Railway, a horse-drawn line built in 1825 and engineered by the Stephenson brothers. This was constructed to carry slate from the quarries at Nantlle to the quayside at Caernarfon.

Pant Glas Station, looking towards Afon Wen, 27 June 1956.

The construction of the 'Town Link' in 1871 made Pant Station redundant and gave the line access to Bangor over the Bangor-Caernarfon branch line. Well patronised in the late 1940s and early 1950s, bringing holidaymakers to Butlin's Holiday Camp at Penychain, the line gradually fell into decline and was closed in 1964. Dinas Station was reactivated for one day on 9 August 1963 for the Royal Train on the occasion of the Queen's visit to Criccieth. It was then closed once more.

Llangybi Station, looking towards Bangor, 27 June 1956.

The track has been relayed in narrow gauge between Caernarfon and Dinas as part of the Festiniog Railway's 'Welsh Highland Railway' project, with a terminus close to the site of the former Pant Station. Between Llanwnda and Pant Glas a great deal of the track is now just a narrow footpath. The building of a new section of the A487, opened in 2001, runs over the former site of Penygroes Station.

Chwilog Station, looking towards Bangor, 27 June 1956.

Caernarfon – Nantlle

Passenger service withdrawn	08/08/1932	*Stations*	*Dates of opening and closure*
Distance	8 miles 343 yards	Nantlle (Talysarn) *	12/1871 – 08/08/1932
Companies	Caernarfonshire Railway; London & North Western; Great Western		

* Closed temporarily between 01/1917 and 07/1919.

Nantlle Station, looking towards the end of the line, 17 July 1963.

When the former Nantlle Railway (built by Robert and George Stephenson) was converted between Penygroes and Caernarfon to standard gauge, the remainder of the line into Nantlle Station and beyond remained as a 3 feet 6 inch gauge horse-drawn line. It was not until 1871 that the line to Nantlle from Penygroes was converted to standard gauge with a new junction on the Afon Wen line just south-east of Penygroes. The line north of Nantlle Station (actually situated in Talysarn) remained 3 feet 6 inch and horse-drawn right up to closure for freight on 3 December 1963, serving the quarries and qualifying as British Railways' only horse-drawn railway. Freight services had begun in 1870.

Caernarfon – Llanberis

		Stations	Dates of opening and closure
Passenger service withdrawn	22/09/1930	Caernarfon (Morfa)	10/1869 – 05/07/1870
Distance	8 miles 1584 yards	Cwm-y-Glo	07/1869 – 22/09/1930
Companies	Caernarfonshire Railway;	Pontrug *	01/06/1880 – 22/09/1930
	London & North Western;	Padarn Halt	21/11/1936 – 09/1969
	Great Western	Llanberis	07/1869 – 22/09/1930
		Pontrhyhalt	10/1869 – 22/09/1930

* Closed temporarily between 01/1917 and 07/1919.

Cwm-y-Glo Station, *c*.1906.

Llanberis Station.

The Caernarfon & Llanberis Railway was built with at least one eye on the lucrative slate, ironstone, copper and sulphur traffic handled by the Padarn Railway. Initially running alongside the Caernarfon – Afon Wen branch, the line diverged after about a mile to Morfa Station, Caernarfon's third station, which was also made redundant and closed by the 'Town Link'. Holiday traffic was sparse and led to closure to passenger trains in 1930, although freight and various specials ran over the line until it was lifted in the 1960s.

Bala Junction – Blaenau Ffestiniog

		Stations	Dates of opening and closure
Passenger service withdrawn	02/01/1960	Arenig	01/11/1882 – 02/01/1960
Distance	22 miles	Cwm Prysor	01/11/1882 – 02/01/1960
Companies	Bala & Festiniog Railway;	Trawsfynydd	01/11/1882 – 04/01/1940
	London & North Western	Trawsfynydd Lake	01/11/1882 – 02/01/1960
		Maentwrog Road	01/11/1882 – 02/01/1960
Stations	*Dates of opening and closure*	Ffestiniog	01/11/1882 – 02/01/1960
Bala Junction	01/11/1882 – 02/01/1960	Teigl	01/11/1882 – 02/01/1960
Bala	01/04/1868 – 18/01/1965	Manod	01/11/1882 – 02/01/1960
Frongoch	01/11/1882 – 02/01/1960	Blaenau Ffestiniog	01/11/1882 – 02/01/1960
Tyddyn Bridge	01/11/1882 – 02/01/1960		
Capel Celyn	01/11/1882 – 02/01/1960		

Engine No. 5810 with the 10.50 a.m. service to Bala at Bala Junction Station, 15 August 1953.

The Bala & Festiniog Railway Company promoted the line from Bala Junction (Llangower) to Ffestiniog by building a standard gauge line from the outskirts of Bala to the Vynfal Valley, where it met end on with the earlier Festiniog and Blaenau narrow gauge line which it converted to standard gauge.

Arenig Station, looking towards Blaenau Ffestiniog, 15 August 1953.

Although freight traffic over the line ceased in 1930, passenger traffic was steady and the line might have survived the Beeching cuts but for the commencement of construction in 1957 of a new reservoir in the Trewern Valley by the Liverpool Waterworks to serve Liverpool. This flooded part of the line and it was closed. Part of the line then formed the road from Bala to Trawsfynnydd.

Cwm Prysor Station, 1950.

The part of the line from Trawfynnydd to Blaenau Ffestiniog remained in use for freight use for many years after the construction of the Trawsfynnydd Nuclear Power Station, carrying nuclear waste up to the Colwyn Valley line for onward transportation until 1995 when the power station closed. The last train carrying nuclear waste ran on 12 August 1995, and although the track has been left in place, it is now disused.

Troops and horses at Trawsfynydd Station, bound for the nearby camp.

Trawsfynydd Lake Halt, 15 August 1953.

Ffestiniog Station, looking towards Blaenau Ffestiniog, 20 March 1959.

Blaenau Ffestiniog Station, looking towards the end of the line, 20 March 1959.

Bangor – Bethesda

		Stations	Dates of opening and closure
Passenger service withdrawn	03/12/1963	Felin Hen	01/07/1884 – 03/12/1951
Distance	4 miles 660 yards	Tregarth	01/07/1884 – 03/12/1951
Company	London & North Western	Bethesda	01/07/1884 – 03/12/1951

Felin Hen Station.

Bethesda Station, 19 July 1963.

The line from Bangor to Bethesda was built largely by public demand, but also in the hope that some of the lucrative slate traffic would come its way. It closely followed the path of the Penrhyn Railway for much of its length. Popular in the 1930s, when up to sixteen trains each way were run, its life was inexplicably linked to the quarries and their decline led to passenger closure on 3 December 1951, except for the occasional special or excursion. Freight services, which had begun on the same date as passenger services, ran until 7 October 1963.

Bala – Dolgellau

Passenger service withdrawn	18/01/1965
Distance	17 miles 440 yards
Company	Bala & Dolgellau Railway; Great Western

Stations	Dates of opening and closure
Bala	01/04/1868 – 18/01/1965
Glan Llyn	04/08/1868 – 18/01/1965
Llanuwchllyn *	04/08/1868 – 18/01/1965

Stations	Dates of opening and closure
Llys Halt	04/08/1868 – 18/01/1965
Garneddwen	09/07/1928 – 18/01/1965
Drws-y-Nant	04/08/1868 – 18/01/1965
Wnion	05/07/1933 – 18/01/1965
Bontnewydd	04/08/1868 – 18/01/1965
Dolserau	08/02/1935 – 29/10/1951
Dollgelley **	04/08/1868 – 18/01/1965

Garneddwen, viewed from the south, 15 July 1963.

* Originally named Pandy until 1870.

** Renamed Dollgellau in 1960.

Drws-y-Nant Station, looking towards Barmouth, 15 July 1963.

The Corwen & Bala Railway reached Bala in 1868. Work had already commenced to extend the line through to Dollgellau and this extension was opened on 4 August 1868. The line included one private halt at Glan Llyn, which was connected with a ferry crossing on Bala Lake to a private residence; it was known as a 'flag' station because the practice was only to stop when a flag was flown at the halt. Today, the Bala Lake Railway runs a narrow gauge service between Bala and Llanuwchllyn along the old trackbed.

Portmadoc engine shed, 12 June 1949.

Barmouth – Dollgellau

Passenger service withdrawn	18/01/1965	*Stations*	*Dates of opening and closure*
Distance	2 miles	Penmaenpool	03/07/1865 – 18/01/1965
Companies	Barmouth & Dollgellau Railway;	Arthog	1870 – 18/01/1965
	Great Western	Morfa Mawddach	03/07/1865 – 18/01/1965
		Barmouth Junction	03/07/1865 – 13/06/1960
Stations	*Dates of opening and closure*	Barmouth	03/07/1865 – still open on
Dollgelley *	04/08/1868 – 18/01/1965		the Cambrian line.

Dolgellau Station, 12 June 1949.

* Renamed Dollgellau in 1960.

Barmouth Station.

The Cambrian Railway's branch to Dollgellau first opened in 1865, but only as far as Penmaenpool. The company was forced into completing the line when the Bala & Dollgellau Railway, anxious to reach the coast, obtained powers to construct the Penmaenpool to Dollgellau section if the Cambrian did not finish by August 1869. Originally the Cambrian had planned their own Dollgellau station but it took a deviation of the Cambrian's planned line to reach a junction with the Bala & Dollgellau and run into the existing station, so providing a through route. This through route just missed out surviving the Beeching cuts when the Cambrian Coast line was retained instead.

The Dinas Mawddwy branch *

		Stations	Dates of opening and closure
Passenger service withdrawn	01/01/1931	Dinas Mawddwy	01/10/1867 – 01/01/1931
Distance	6 miles 1320 yards	Mallwyd	1896 – 17/04/1901
Company	Mawddwy Railway;	Aberangell	01/10/1867 – 01/01/1931
	Cambrian Railway;	Cemaes	29/07/1911 – 01/01/1931
	Great Western	Cemaes Road	01/10/1867 – 17/04/1901

Dinas Mawddwy Station, 25 July 1904.

* All stations on this branch were temporarily closed between 17/04/1901 and 29/07/1911.

Cemaes Road Station.

The line from Dinas Mawddwy to Cemaes Road was built at the expense of Sir Edmund Buckley, the local landowner, who felt that agriculture and quarrying around Dinas Mawddwy were losing out by the town's lack of railway communication. Passenger traffic was disappointing from the outset, although heavily promoted for angling along the River Dovey. Freight traffic fared little better. This standard gauge line was closed twice, once to passengers in 1901 and freight in 1908 when its wooden bridges were deemed unsafe. Reopened in 1911, it survived until closed by flooding in 1948, although passenger services had ceased in 1931. Freight services ran from 1 October 1867 to 8 April 1908 and from 29 July 1911 to 20 August 1948.

The North Wales Narrow Gauge main line

Passenger service withdrawn	10/1916		
Distance	7 miles 440 yards		
Company	North Wales Narrow Gauge Railways		

Stations	*Dates of opening and closure*	*Stations*	*Dates of opening and closure*
Dinas Junction	15/08/1877 – 10/1916	Bettws Garmon	15/08/1877 – 10/1916
Tryfan Junction	15/08/1877 – 10/1916	Salem Halt	15/08/1877 – 10/1916
Waenfawr	15/08/1877 – 10/1916	Plas-y-Nant Halt	15/08/1877 – 10/1916
		Quellyn Lake	15/08/1877 – 10/1916
		Snowdon Ranger	15/08/1877 – 10/1916
		Rhyd-Ddu	15/08/1877 – 10/1916

0-6-4ST engine 'Beddgelert' at Dinas Junction, *c.*1905. The engine was scrapped in 1906.

The derelict station building at Waenfawr, 1 November 1947.

This line was part of the North Wales Narrow Gauge Railways' grandiose scheme to provide a network of narrow gauge lines linking Porthmadog, Beddgelert, Bettws-y-Coed, Corwen, Penmachno and Pwllheli. In the event only two sections of the original plan were built, from Dinas Junction to Rhyd-Ddu and from Dinas to Bryngwyn. The line was in financial trouble even before it opened and it was placed in receivership in 1878, although the section between Snowdon Ranger and Rhyd-Ddu was not opened until 1881!

The line struggled on, surviving one crisis after another until 1923, when it became part of the Welsh Highland Railway. Passenger traffic was suspended in 1916 because of the First World War. Freight traffic, however, was continuous to July 1922 from the sections to Quellyn Lake from 21 May 1877, from Snowdon Ranger from 1 June 1878 and from Rhyd-Ddu from 14 May 1881. Rhyd-Ddu was also named South Snowdon and Snowdon during its lifetime.

The North Wales Narrow Gauge: Bryngwyn branch

Passenger service withdrawn	10/1916	*Stations*	*Dates of opening and closure*
Distance	5 miles 220 yards	Dinas Junction	15/08/1877 – 10/1916
Company	North Wales Narrow Gauge Railways	Tryfan Junction	15/08/1877 – 10/1916
		Rhostryfan	08/1877 – 10/1916
		Bryngwyn	08/1877 – 10/1916

Bryngwyn Station.

The North Wales Narrow Gauge line from Dinas Junction to Bryngwyn was the main reason both this and their main line were built. At Bryngwyn an incline connected it with lines running from quarries above Nantlle and the valuable slate trade. Passenger services ceased due to the war in 1916, never to resume even in Welsh Highland Railway days and freight services came within an inch of ceasing in 1906 when the only locomotive capable of dealing with the branches heavy gradients, 'Beddgelert', was in such poor condition it had to be scrapped. It was only when the Porthmadog, Beddgelert & South Snowdon Railway purchased 'Russell', a Hunslet locomotive capable of handling the gradients, that they were able to continue.

The Croesor Tramway

Distance   4 miles   *Company*   The Croesor Tramway

The Croesor Tramway was built under a system of wayleaves in 1864, although there is evidence that it may have been in use a year earlier. Built to convey slate to Porthmadog from the Croesor quarries and flour, coal and other goods back, it was horse-drawn and remained so between Croesor Junction and Croesor even in Welsh Highland Railway days, which commenced in 1923 after the Croesor Railway was re-laid and converted to steam. An Act of Parliament authorised the tramway to carry passengers on 5 July 1865, but it never did so.

Porthmadog, Beddgelert & South Snowdon Railway

The Porthmadog, Beddgelert & South Snowdon Railway was formed to connect the Croesor Tramway and the North Wales Narrow Gauge lines to provide a through route from Porthmadog to Dinas Junction via Beddgelert, providing access to the then important ports of Caernarfon and Porthmadog to the slate trade. It purchased one engine, 'Russell', to enable the North Wales Narrow Gauge to survive and did various construction work in the Beddgelert area, including the bridge over the road entering Beddgelert, which never saw a train, before running out of money.

The engine 'Russell' at Dinas Junction.

The Welsh Highland Light Railway

Passenger service withdrawn	26/09/1936
Distance	21 miles
Company	The Welsh Highland Light Railway

Stations	*Dates of opening and closure*
Dinas Junction	31/07/1922 – 26/09/1936
Tryfan Junction	31/07/1922 – 26/09/1936

Stations	*Dates of opening and closure*
Waenfawr	31/07/1922 26/09/1936
Bettws Garmon	31/07/1922 – 26/09/1936
Salem Halt	31/07/1922 – 26/09/1936
Plas-y-Nant Halt	31/07/1922 – 26/09/1936
Snowdon Ranger	31/07/1922 – 26/09/1936
South Snowdon	31/07/1922 – 26/09/1936

The 0-6-4T engine 'Moel Tryfan' at South Snowdon Station.

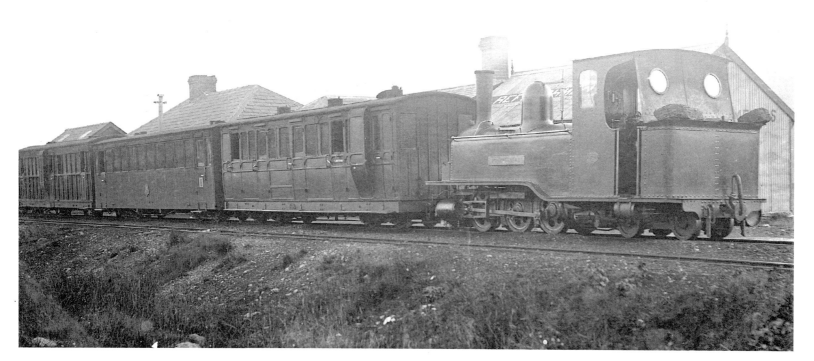

The Welsh Highland Light Railway (continued)

Stations	*Dates of opening and closure*	*Stations*	*Dates of opening and closure*
Pitts Head Halt	01/06/1923 – 26/09/1966	Croesor Junction	01/06/1923 – 26/09/1966
Hafod Ruffydd Halt	01/06/1923 – 26/09/1966	Ynysfor	01/06/1923 – 26/09/1966
Beddgelert	01/06/1923 – 26/09/1966	Pont Croesor	01/06/1923 – 26/09/1966
Nantmor *	01/06/1923 – 26/09/1966	Porthmadog New	01/06/1923 – 26/09/1966
Hafod-y-Llyn Halt	01/06/1923 – 26/09/1966	Porthmadog New (1933) **	07/1933 – 09/1936
Hafod Garregog Halt	01/06/1923 – 26/09/1966		

Beddgelert Station, 1923.

BEDDGELERT STATION, WELSH HIGHLAND RAILWAY.   88230 J.V.

* Also known as Aberglaslyn.   ** Built in 1933 to the west of Porthmadog New Station to avoid costs of crossing the Cambrian Railways line. Passengers would alight here, cross the Cambrian tracks and join a Ffestiniog train at Porthmadog New to journey to the Ffestiniog Harbour Station.

Nantmor Station.

The Welsh Highland Railway finally provided the desired link between Porthmadog and Dinas Junction in 1923, heavily subsidised by the Board of Trade and local councils. The line was unsuccessful, however, as motor transport had already begun to assert its ascendancy and the line's habit of running passenger trains only during the summer months did not endear it to locals.

The Porthmadog New Station of 1923.

The line fell into receivership in 1927 and despite the Festiniog Railway leasing the line in 1934 and promoting it for holiday excursions, the summer 1936 season was its last, although the final train ran in 1937. Today the Festiniog Railway is reviving it from the north while the Welsh Highland Railway work from the south.

Porthmadog New Station (1933), 9 October 1948.

Gorseddau Tramway

Distance   Porthmadog – Gorseddau Quarry: 8 miles 880 yards; Gorseddau Quarry – Braich-y-Bib: 11 miles
Companies   Bangor & Porthmadog Slate & Slab Company; Gorseddau Junction & Porthmadog Railway

The Gorsedau Tramway was built in the 1850s to connect the Gorseddau slate quarry with Porthmadog, using in part a much earlier line between Tremadog and Porthmadog. Horse-drawn until 1872, when the line was extended from Braich-y-Bib, just north of the Slate Mill at Ynys-y-Pandy, to the head of the Pennant Valley and the Cwm Dwyfor silver, lead and copper mines and the New Prince of Wales slate quarry, at which time locomotives were introduced. Neither venture proved profitable, however, and the line fell into disuse in the 1890s.

Moel-y-Gest Tramway

Distance   1,320 yards   *Company*   Borth Stone Company

Dates for the Moel-y-Gest Tramway have been lost in the mists of time, but it would appear that this ran from around 1880 until the closure of the Gorseddau Tramway as it used part of this to take slate to Porthmadog. A vertical boilered De Winton locomotive was used, said to have come from the New Prince of Wales quarry on the Gorseddau line.

The Penrhyn Railway

		Stations	Dates of opening and closure
Passenger service withdrawn	09/02/1951	Quay Siding	01/07/1801 – 09/02/1951
Distance	6 miles 440 yards	Tregarth	01/07/1801 – 09/02/1951
Company	Penrhyn Railway	Felin Hen	01/07/1801 – 09/02/1951
		Penrhyn Quarry	01/07/1801 – 09/02/1951

The 0-4-0ST engine 'Blanche' on the Penrhyn Railway with a workmen's train, 22 July 1947.

The Penrhyn Railway was the first railway in Gwynedd, connecting the quarries at Bethesda (principally the Penrhyn Quarry) with Port Penrhyn where loading onto ships was possible (and later onto standard gauge trains). Horse-drawn until 1877, when part of the line was re-sited to avoid the necessity of inclines and to enable locomotive traction to be used, the narrow gauge track was principally freight operated although 'Workman's Specials' were run on Monday mornings and Saturday afternoons to convey the workers to and from the quarries and their homes. The line finally closed on 24 July 1962, a result of the run down of the quarries.

The Corris Tramway

		Stations	Dates of opening and closure
Passenger service withdrawn	01/01/1931	Corris	04/07/1883 – 01/01/1931
Distance	5 miles 440 yards	Aberllefenni	25/08/1887 – 01/01/1931
Company	Corris, Machynlleth & River Dovey Tramway; Great Western	Machynlleth	04/07/1883 – 01/01/1931

Corris Station, May 1941.

0-4-0ST No. 2 at Machynlleth Station, 1906.

The Corris Railway was built to service the slate quarries at Aberllefenni and Corris in the Dulas Valley. Built in narrow gauge as the Corris, Machynlleth & River Dovey Tramway in 1859, the line survived for freight until 1948 when flooding closed the line, it having been in GWR hands from 1930. Passenger traffic lasted a significantly shorter time. Today the Corris Railway Society has a small museum devoted to the line and plans to open a section from Corris to Llwyngwern.

0-4-2ST No. 2, 'Falcon', at Aberllefeni Station.

The Trefor Tramway

The quarries at Trefor built two lines in the late nineteenth century, one down the hillside to the centre of the village for transhipment of its product to road transport, the other leading to the seashore and a pier for loading ships. The lines fell into disuse and were lifted in the 1920s.

The Padarn Railway

Passenger service withdrawn	27/10/1961		
Distance	7 miles		
Company	The Padarn Railway		
		Stations	*Dates of opening and closure*
		Crawia	01/05/1895 – 27/10/1961
Stations	*Dates of opening and closure*	Pensarn	01/05/1895 – 27/10/1961
Dinorwic Quarry	03/03/1843 – 27/10/1961	Bethel	03/03/1843 – 27/10/1961
Penllyn	01/05/1895 – 27/10/1961	Cefn Gwyn	01/05/1895 – 27/10/1961
Pontrhythallt	03/03/1843 – 27/10/1961	Penscoins	01/05/1895 – 27/10/1961
		Port Dinorwic	03/03/1843 – 27/10/1961

Pontrhythallt Station, looking towards Llanberis, 10 June 1949.

The Padarn Railway was built in 1825 as a 2 feet gauge horse-drawn railway. This was re-laid in 1848, in 4 feet gauge and on a slightly different route to avoid the inclines which previously had been necessary. It continued as a horse-drawn railway until 1864 when it became locomotive powered. Running alongside the lake at Llanberis, it ran from the Dinorwic Quarry via Pontrhythallt and Bethel to Port Dinorwic, where the slate was loaded onto ships and later, when the Standard Gauge arrived, onto trains. Essentially freight, workmen's trains ran regularly between 1895 and 1945. Falling demand and production meant the end of the line and it closed on the 27 October 1961. The route alongside the lake has been reopened as a 2 feet gauge tourist railway, the Llanberis Lake Railway.

The Pwllheli – Llanbedrog Tramway

Passenger service withdrawn	28/10/1927	*Stations*	*Dates of opening and closure*
Distance	3 miles 1320 yards	West End	21/05/1894 – 28/10/1927
Company	Solomon Andrews & Co. Ltd	Carreg-y-Defaid	21/05/1894 – 28/10/1927
		Glyn-y-Weddw	01/08/1896 – 28/10/1927

West End, Pwllheli.

The Pwllheli – Llanbedrog Tramway was laid by Solomon Andrews, initially to bring stone from the Carreg-y-Defaid Quarry to Pwllheli in order to build his estate on land at West End in 1893. When this proved popular as a means of transport with locals coming into Pwllheli for market days, he purchased the Glyn-y-Weddw Estate at Llanbedrog and extended the tramway there, where he ran afternoon tea dances for holidaymakers. The line was destroyed twice by storms, once in 1898, but re-laid that year, and again in 1927. The latter occasion caused the closure of the line. The tramway was horse-drawn throughout its life.

The Cardiff Road Tramway

Passenger service withdrawn	31/03/1928	*Stations*	*Dates of opening and closure*
Distance	1 mile	Cardiff Road	29/08/1896 – 31/03/1928
Company	Solomon Andrews & Co. Ltd	West End	29/08/1896 – 31/03/1928

The Cardiff Road Tramway was another of Solomon Andrews horse-drawn lines. Originally he had wanted to run a line from Maes Square, Pwllheli, near the railway station, to Pwllheli West End, but was blocked by the town council. In 1896 he then built the Cardiff Road line, running down the aforesaid road on his own land (which the council had no control over) to his hotel at Pwllheli Road. Despite its closeness to his other line, there was apparently no connection between the two. The line closed in 1928 when the council adopted Cardiff Road and laid electricity cables alongside the road.

The horse-tram at Pwllheli, 1906.

The Pwllheli Corporation Tramway

Passenger service withdrawn	16/09/1919	*Stations*	*Dates of opening and closure*
Distance	880 yards	Station Square	24/07/1899 – 16/09/1919
Company	Pwllheli Corporation	South Beach	24/07/1899 – 16/09/1919

The Pwllheli Corporation Tramway, opened in 1898, ran from outside the present Pwllheli Station to the South End Hotel (destroyed by fire in 1937). It really only came into full usage when Pwllheli Station was moved from its former position on the far eastern side of the town to its present location. Built of flimsy second-hand (some say ex-quarry) rail, its end came in 1919 when the track was declared to be in too poor a condition for it to continue and replacement rail proved impossible to locate at a reasonable price.